VIVA CAREER SKILLS LIBRARY

Professional Ethics and Etiquette

Second Edition

VIVA CAREER SKILLS LIBRARY

Professional Ethics and Etiquette

SECOND EDITION

Viva Books

New Delhi | Mumbai | Chennai | Kolkata | Bangalore | Hyderabad | Kochi

First Indian Edition 2007
Reprinted 2008

VIVA BOOKS PRIVATE LIMITED

- 4737/23 Ansari Road, Daryaganj, New Delhi 110 002
  E-mail: vivadelhi@vivagroupindia.net, Tel. 42242200
- 76, Service Industries, Shirvane, Sector 1, Nerul, Navi Mumbai 400 706
  E-mail: vivamumbai@vivagroupindia.net, Tel. 27721273, 27721274
- Jamals Fazal Chambers, 26 Greams Road, Chennai 600 006
  E-mail: vivachennai@vivagroupindia.net, Tel. 28290304, 28294241
- B-103, Jindal Towers, 21/1A/3 Darga Road, Kolkata 700 017
  E-mail: vivakolkata@vivagroupindia.net, Tel. 22836381, 22816713
- 7, Sovereign Park Apartments, 56-58, K. R. Road, Basavanagudi, Bangalore 560 004
  E-mail: vivabangalore@vivagroupindia.net, Tel. 26607409, 26607410
- 101-102 Mughal Marc Apartments, 3-4-637 to 641, Narayanguda, Hyderabad 500 029
  E-mail: vivahyderabad@vivagroupindia.net, Tel. 27564481, 27564482
- Beevi Towers, First Floor, SRM Road, Kaloor, Kochi 682 018, Kerala
  E-mail: vivakochi@vivagroupindia.net, Tel: 0484-2403055, 2403056

www.vivagroupindia.com

Published by arrangement with

Facts on File, Inc.
132 West 31st Street
New York NY 10001
USA

ISBN-10: 81-309-0355-5
ISBN-13: 978-81-309-0355-2

Published by Vinod Vasishtha for Viva Books Private Limited, 4737/23, Ansari Road, New Delhi-110 002. Printed and bound by Raj Press, R-3, Inderpuri, New Delhi - 110 012

CONTENTS

INTRODUCTION

From coast to coast, employers search for the ideal employee. Skills and experience count, but most businesses are looking for something else, too: character.

The kind of person you are matters to your employer. One of the most important things you can do right now for your career is to develop the type of character that employers want. How responsible are you? Are you the kind of person others can count on? Have you developed good habits such as working hard, striving for excellence, and practicing professional etiquette? It's never too early or too late to develop these qualities.

Great management is about character, not technique

—Thomas Teal, *Harvard Business Review*

This book begins with your favorite subject—you. You'll unlock the secrets of your temperament, your learning style, your strengths and weaknesses, and your values. Then you'll take an honest look at what employers want to see in you when you show up for work. You'll get tips on everything from how to manage your time to improving your memory. You'll learn to develop your personal code of ethics and maintain a professional presence.

In other words, you're about to discover that your best secret weapon to a successful career could be you.

The most important thing for a young man [woman] is to establish a credit—a reputation, character.

—John D. Rockefeller, American businessman

This book covers the following topics:

- Learning about yourself so you can identify which areas of your professional life need the most improvement
- Getting in touch with your personal values and ethics so you know how to react to various situations
- Becoming a responsible person that others can count on

- Acting professionally in all situations—from appropriate dress code to after-hours etiquette
- Making an impact on others by being aggressively nice
- Asking questions and learning the ropes at a new job
- Improving your memory through word association and other techniques
- Balancing your work life and avoiding job stress

1

GAIN SELF-KNOWLEDGE

Self-knowledge is definitely "in." People pay analysts thousands of dollars to learn more about themselves. Books on self-image and self-improvement are always among the best-sellers. Several psychologists have become national radio and television celebrities. Most of us spend more time thinking, worrying, and dreaming about ourselves than we spend on all other subjects combined.

Focusing on self-knowledge can be invaluable as you pursue a career. Although employers look for specific technical skills and abilities in job candidates, character counts.

A NEW YOU

If you're just beginning your career, you're on the verge of becoming a whole new person. Talk to people who have recently graduated and started careers. Most of them will have stories of how much they've changed because of their work environments.

Michele got a first-year teaching job as coach at a state special-education school. As she talks about her experiences, she shakes her head, still amazed at what she learned about herself. "I thought I was pretty together. But I didn't have a clue how I'd react to so much responsibility. Nothing in school prepared me for being in charge of so much. I thought I was pretty outgoing, but all I wanted to do was retreat—hide out."

Ben discovered new things about himself when he joined a group of trainees as part of a telecommunications company. He admits, "I would have said I was pretty mature. But three months of training really threw me. I didn't think I was an emotional person, but I went up and down, highs and lows—all over the emotional map. I didn't know what was going on."

Be more concerned with your character than your reputation, because your character is what you really are, while your reputation is merely what others think you are.

—John Wooden, former basketball coach and member of the Basketball Hall of Fame

Meredith took a job as part of a secretarial pool in a large investment firm. She started getting depressed her first week at work. Everybody else seemed outgoing and excited about the new challenges. Meredith dreaded every change. Then she remembered some of the material she'd read on personality types.

"In one of my classes, we took personality tests. I came out the type who is reliable, but doesn't like new things. So I knew that what may have come naturally for my coworkers just didn't for me. But that was okay. I could do what I needed to socially. At the same time, I could make myself indispensable by using my strengths. I didn't have to try to imitate their strengths."

Former basketball coach John Wooden stressed that having a strong character is more important than having a popular reputation. As you gain self-knowledge, you will learn how to strengthen your character. (Corbis)

KNOW YOURSELF

Now is the right time for you to get to know yourself. Self-knowledge won't make all the surprises and stresses of your first year on the job go away, but you'll be better prepared for those changes and better able to understand your own reactions.

If you can learn more about yourself, you can equip yourself for your career. For example, if you know that your energy can be "refueled" only when you're alone, you know to plan time to be by yourself. If you're aware of your laid-back tendencies, you know to give yourself an occasional go-ahead kick.

Knowing yourself gives you a chance to meet your own needs. That takes pressure off at work. Then, if your job doesn't meet your expectations, your whole world won't fall apart.

FACT

Noted psychologist Carl R. Rogers claimed that self-discovery is the basis of psychological health and success. After treating thousands of patients, he concluded that one central issue lies behind almost every problem—a lack of self-knowledge.

PROFILES AND TYPES

When you say that someone has a great personality, what do you mean? How about when you refer to someone who's "not your type"? Psychologists generally refer to personality and type by certain categories. Many of these categories are based on opposite characteristics: introvert/extrovert; feeling/thinking; perceiving/judging; sensing/intuiting.

People seem to be born with tendencies toward specific temperaments, learning styles, and thinking styles. No one style is the right one or even the preferable one. But if you know your styles and your temperament, you can use your strengths in work situations—and can be on guard against your potential weaknesses.

PERSONALITY

Each personality is completely unique, but many have common characteristics that can be grouped together. In the Middle Ages, physicians divided the temperaments of personalities into four categories: phlegmatic, sanguine, choleric, and melancholy. Many variations exist among the categories, and nobody fits completely into one of the categories. Yet most of us can easily see ourselves in one or two of these four divisions.

The following exercise is a personality inventory to give you clues as you investigate who you are. The exercise is designed to give you an idea about personality for entertainment purposes. For more

EXERCISE

Four categories of personality traits are given in the chart to the right. Divide a sheet of paper into four quarters. Mark one quarter with a P (for phlegmatic) at the top, one with an S (for sanguine), one with a C (for choleric), and one with an M (for melancholy). Under each letter, write the words or phrases from the corresponding quarters of the chart that describe you most of the time.

accurate information, and a much more thorough inventory, ask your school counselor to give you the Meyer-Briggs Type Indicator or any of the more scientific inventories your school recommends.

APPLYING YOUR KNOWLEDGE OF PERSONALITY

Look over your sheet from the above exercise. Are there more words under one personality type than the others? To get another perspective, ask a parent, sibling, or friend to do this inventory according to

CATEGORIES OF PERSONALITY TRAITS

Phlegmatic

easygoing
discerning
uninvolved
not bossy
consistent
spectator
stubborn
accurate
detailed
pleasant
submissive
rarely angry
dry humor
kindhearted
indecisive
orderly
calm
adjusts well
reserved
steady
can be lazy
can imitate others
fearful
predictable
laid-back
factual
timid
sleepy
scheduled
peacemaker
analytical
controlled

Sanguine

laughs a lot
conceited
optimistic
enthusiastic
inspirational
friendly
poor listener
dislikes being alone
likes new things
bubbly
verbal
likes taking risks
spontaneous
fun-loving
popular
lacks follow-through
outgoing
pleasant
adventurous
initiator
makes others laugh
likes change
gets bored easily
shallow relationships
angry
smiles a lot
visionary
motivator
energetic
talkative
forgets easily

Choleric

domineering
impudent
logical
active
confident
controlled
poor listener
enterprising
purposeful
hard to discourage
determined
quarrelsome
angry
decisive
inflexible
ambitious
goal-oriented
good planner
problem solver
handles pressure well
leader
demanding
strong-willed
likes a challenge
impatient
pushy
well organized
self-reliant
opinionated
hot-tempered
practical
independent
competitive
insensitive
stubborn
firm
adventurous
brave

Melancholy

analytical
creative
moody
shy
visionary
pessimistic
gifted
hypochondria
genius tendencies
self-sacrificing
individualistic
intense
suspicious
self-centered
critical
fearful
private
may be depressed
perfectionist
emotional
faithful friend
thinks "too much"
sensitive
vengeful
sad
hurt feelings
artsy
introvert
dependable
slow to initiate
feels guilty
solitary
imaginative

their perception of you. These inventories are designed to get you thinking about your personality type. For more detailed analysis, ask your guidance counselor.

Each of the four temperaments, or personality types, carries with it a set of strengths and corresponding weaknesses. If you wrote most of your words and phrases under one category, pay special attention to the tendencies of that temperament.

Phlegmatic

The phlegmatic may need to be on guard against laziness or a lack of motivation.

Life for the phlegmatic-type person tends to go along smoothly. Her strengths lie in her combination of abilities and her steady consistency. She can relax, enjoy friends, and keep the peace. She's easy to live with and undemanding. The phlegmatic may need to be on guard against laziness or a lack of motivation that keeps her on the sidelines as a spectator. She can become stubborn, indecisive, and even fearful.

Melancholy

The melancholic-type person sees things in life that others miss. He's sensitive and often gifted. He doesn't mind sacrificing himself for others and makes a faithful friend and a good listener. He is thoughtful of others. He's always dependable because his perfectionist tendencies make him conscious of letting people down.

The sanguine personality type is generally happy and energetic at work. (Corbis)

The melancholic may need to work on controlling his moods, which can vary widely with his emotions. He needs to stand up for himself and make tough decisions. He may have to work on meeting new people and not worrying what others think about him.

Sanguine

A sanguine temperament is great in a crowd. She loves new situations and experiences and is seldom at a loss for words. She's cheerful, enthusiastic, and a great motivator, full of energy. The sanguine person may need to improve her organization and follow-through. She should work on becoming a better listener and on

Sanguines tend to get bored easily and become restless and undisciplined.

forming deeper relationships. Sanguines tend to get bored easily and become restless and undisciplined.

Choleric

The choleric is independent, decisive, and self-sufficient. He has little trouble making decisions and usually makes a strong leader. He loves activity and has lots of ideas and the plans to implement them. He's determined, practical, and knows his own mind.

The choleric may be so goal-oriented that he'll need to be careful not to overlook other people's needs. He can be a tough person to live with, inflexible, and impatient. He may need to work on people skills to become a motivator rather than a dictator.

LEARNING STYLES

You've probably heard about recent studies on how our brains function. The brain has two sides, and each hemisphere functions differently. Most of us depend more on one side of the brain than the other as we learn new information. In part, that explains our different learning styles.

For example, you want to give your little sister a tricycle for Christmas. Christmas Eve comes, and it's time to assemble the pieces. Do you pull out the instruction book and read through it step-by-step? Or do you dump everything out on the living room car-

BRAIN HEMISPHERE DOMINANCE

Left-Brain Learner	Right-Brain Learner
Sees in parts	Sees the whole
Logical	Creative
Learns in numbered steps	Learns by figuring out
Follows in straight line	Sees the pattern
Likes words	Likes images
Orderly, organized	Spontaneous

pet and start figuring what goes where? What you do says a lot about your learning style.

Some of us are more "left-brained," or analytical, in the way we learn. We need the instruction book and well-ordered steps. The left side of the brain handles numbers, words, and details. It's organized and sequential. The left brain analyzes parts.

"Right-brained" people see the whole picture. They remember faces (forget the names), patterns, and images. Give them a vision of what's needed, and let them create spontaneously. They'll get that tricycle together eventually. Forget the instruction book.

Another difference in learning style is whether we learn more effectively through hearing (auditory), seeing and writing (visual), or touching (kinesthetic). The auditory learner learns best from word of mouth. Verbal instruction has the most impact—hearing someone's name, listening to instructions.

The visual learner tends to think in pictures and remember what she sees or writes. Hearing directions doesn't work as well as putting those directions in writing.

A kinesthetic learner prefers to learn by doing. Reading or hearing isn't as effective for him as hands-on instruction. Touch is important to the learning process.

APPLYING YOUR KNOWLEDGE OF LEARNING STYLES

Just think about the way you learn best in class. Does it help you to write and rewrite dates or words in order to learn them? Or are you better off saying them aloud? Do you remember more by listening intently to your teacher (auditory), or by taking notes or reading the information in a book (visual)? Are flash cards and other hands-on learning activities most helpful for remembering and learning (kinesthetic)?

Understanding your learning style can help you make a smoother transition to your new job. Imagine your first week on the job. How can you learn and remember names, duties, operations, and procedures? If you're a visual learner, it may help to carry a notebook and record new information and names. Auditory learners can discuss procedures and repeat names aloud. Kinesthetic learners might practice new procedures immediately or take notes and make their own study sheets later. They can look for hands-on tutorials.

FACT

A new tool to aid visual learners is on the market—the SMART Board Interactive Whiteboard. This is a large white screen designed for classroom use to project images from a computer. It can also be used like a blackboard for drawing. Anything created on the SMART Board screen can be saved, printed, or emailed. The screen is also touch-sensitive—teachers can simply press the surface to control applications. To learn more, visit the SMART Technologies website (http://www.smarttech.com).

If you're a left-brain learner, you may want to organize your own steps for new procedures. If you're a right-brain learner, write down names to go with the faces you remember. Your notes might include sketches and patterns.

Pay attention to what works for you now in your classes. This way, you will be ready to make the most out of your learning style when you start your career.

INTROVERTS AND EXTROVERTS

You may already feel you know whether you're an extrovert or an introvert. In general, extroverts are outgoing, like the sanguine personality type. They do well in crowds and enjoy meeting new people. Extroverts tend to be talkers and doers, looking for the action, thriving on activity.

Introverts are thought to be quieter, more private people. They may be shy and more comfortable with the familiar. They enjoy deep friendships and the company of a few good friends, but crowds make them uncomfortable and they retreat.

Still, recent studies have pointed out a significant difference in the categories. Some people may simply be good at faking extroversion, even to themselves. They feel somehow responsible that others have a good time and behave as the life of the party to ensure its success. They have mastered speech and verbal skills and the art of storytelling. All these qualities lead them to believe they are extroverts.

But the truth is that some of these supposed extroverts are in reality introverts. They're just good performers. A more reliable indicator may be your answer to this question: How do you refuel your energy? When you're with a crowd all day or night, do you become energized? Do you gain an energy that takes you into the next day? If so, you are probably the extrovert you believe yourself to be.

Some people may simply be good at faking extroversion, even to themselves.

However, even though you handle yourself well in a crowd, do you refuel only when you're alone? Do you need to be off by yourself to get your head together or get your energy back? If so, you are probably more of an introvert who has learned to be good in a crowd.

What difference does it make whether you're an introvert or an extrovert? Neither is better. But if you understand yourself, you can help yourself ease into your new job. For example, if you're an introvert, take some of your breaks or lunches alone. Use your time at home to refuel. Recognize your need for that alone-time and schedule it. You might need to push yourself to speak up in meetings and to get to know your work team.

If you're an extrovert, volunteer for speaking assignments or events where you can use your social skills. But be careful to use those social skills wisely. It's up to you to monitor your enthusiasm and share the spotlight. You'll want to check yourself in meetings to make sure you don't talk too much. Be careful not to infringe on others' work time by stopping for conversation too often.

BOOKS TO READ

Balzano, Frederica et al. *Why Should Extroverts Make All the Money?: Networking Made Easy for the Introvert.* New York: McGraw-Hill Contemporary Books, 2000.

Camenson, Blythe. *Careers for Introverts and Other Solitary Types.* New York: McGraw-Hill Contemporary Books, 1998.

Laney, Marty Olsen. *The Introvert Advantage: How to Thrive in an Extrovert World.* New York: Workman Publishing Company, 2002.

It is important to know yourself and be aware of your habits and skills. Gaining a solid knowledge of who you are is one of the most important steps of professional development.

You should come up with many more strengths and weaknesses than appear in this example. Get input from friends, family, teachers—anyone who might help you get a clearer understanding of yourself. For each weakness, ask yourself if the flip side might be a strength. For example, if you have trouble making friends (weakness), are you a faithful friend to the ones you have (strength)?

EXERCISES

1. For each type or category that follows, write down where you see yourself. In a sentence or two, explain your choice.

   A. Temperament (phlegmatic, sanguine, choleric, melancholy)

   B. Learning style (left-brain, right-brain)

   C. Learning style (auditory, visual, kinesthetic)

   D. Social (introvert, extrovert)

2. Take a minute and compile a list of strengths and weaknesses.

	Strengths	**Weaknesses**
By myself	content organized	lazy easily bored
With others	make friends easily can make others laugh	don't speak up too critical
At work/school	earn Bs consistent	should earn As don't work hard
Skills/talents	music writing	math mechanical
Miscellaneous	lots of ideas	messy

IN SUMMARY . . .

- One of the most important steps of self-development is learning about yourself—your personality type, your learning style, your skills, strengths, and weaknesses.
- Introverts are shy and private, while extroverts are outgoing and love crowds.
- There are two learning types: right-brain learners and left-brain learners. Right-brain learners use patterns to learn, and they are spontaneous. Left-brain learners are logical and prefer to follow numbered steps.
- There are four temperaments: choleric, sanguine, melancholy, and phlegmatic. Each category represents a different set of personal characteristics, and most of us fit into one or two of these categories.
- Learning styles include visual, auditory, and kinesthetic. Different teaching methods, such as flash cards and films, aid each type of learner.
- Gaining self-knowledge will help you succeed in the workplace, at social events, and in all other areas of your life.

2

RECOGNIZE YOUR VALUES AND ETHICS

Juanita had been working as an editorial assistant for just two hours when she faced her first ethical dilemma. Her boss asked her to lie. "If anyone calls for me," he said, "tell them I've left for the day. I've got to get caught up on work."

Juanita had always thought of herself as an honest person. How could she lie? On the other hand, she'd only been on the job for two hours. How could she challenge her boss? What would you do if you were Juanita?

WHAT'S IMPORTANT TO YOU?

Values are the things and principles that are most important to us. Values involve our feelings, ideas, and beliefs. Whether you're aware of it or not, you operate according to a system of values. Everything you do, every decision you make, comes from inside you—from your own (conscious or unconscious) system of values.

The following is an example of how values might come into play if you are considering dropping an advanced English class. Which one sounds more like you?

- Yes, I should drop the course. My social life is too important to spend that much time reading. This is my senior year and I don't want to miss out on time with my friends. I can't pass that course without cutting back on TV. That course would lower my grade point average and maybe I couldn't play basketball.
- No, I cannot drop the course. I need the course for college. I like literature. My best friend is taking that class. Everybody who's going on to college will take it, and I don't want kids to think I'm not going to college. My parents will flip if I don't take the course.

It's not hard to make decisions when you know what your values are.

—Roy Disney, American film producer and nephew of Walt Disney

You make choices all day and probably never stop to think about your values. Nevertheless, your values are in place and at work all the time. At school, you're used to the possibilities and consequences of most choices. But what about when you start a new career? How will you know what to choose when, like Juanita, you face a tough decision?

Now is the time to get a handle on your values. Know yourself well. Then, when you have to choose, you'll have a better understanding of what's at stake. When Juanita's boss told her to lie and say he was out of the office, she panicked. Many receptionists and assistants face that situation with an "Okay, Boss." They hardly give it a thought. But Juanita knew herself well enough to understand she could not just say "okay." Juanita's parents and her experiences had made her value honesty highly. Trembling, she asked to talk with her employer. Instead of telling him she didn't want to lie for him, Juanita offered an alternative she could live with.

"Mr. Johnson," she said, "would it be all right if I told callers you couldn't come to the phone or that you were unavailable and could I take a message?" He looked at her a moment, and Juanita wondered if she'd have the shortest employment on record.

Then he said, "Sure, that's fine."

Clearly defined values will aid you in everything you do. In an important sense, your crystallized values serve as banisters on a staircase, to guide you, to be touched when you have to make decisions, and in very risky matters, grasped.

—Eugene Raudsepp in *Growth Games for the Creative Manager*

Ideally, in your career, you'll make decisions according to your values. But if you're not aware of your own values, you can expect confusion. A good knowledge of personal values will help you take responsibility for your decisions and your career.

OBSERVE YOURSELF

How well do you know yourself on the inside? Do you make your decisions according to what you think is most important? Do you think you're unselfish, polite, respectful, generous, and honest?

Try starting a journal of self-observations. For one week, see what you can discover about your values. Observe yourself and the reactions you get from others. Pay attention to the value system that's at work in everything you do. It may or may not match the values you think you have. The more you know about yourself, the more control you can have over your value system.

ONE STUDENT'S SELF-OBSERVATION JOURNAL

Monday

This morning before the first bell rang I noticed I talked to three kids only, and I know all of them really well. Am I unfriendly? I also made a point to greet Tom because he's the leader, the most popular in our class. I guess it's important to me to be popular, too.

Mr. B., my science teacher, likes me. His class is the only one where I voluntarily choose a front-row seat. Why? I do want to go to college. That's important to me. His class could make a difference in my getting into a good college. Plus, he's friends with my dad. I value what Dad thinks about me, although I wouldn't admit that to anybody, especially Mr. B. . . . or Dad.

It seems that J. is always getting upset with me. Why? Should I ask her? I value our friendship. But it doesn't stop me from talking about her to Tom. Does that mean I value his popularity more than her friendship?

K. tells me everything and says that I'm easy to talk to. Why? What signals do I give off? Being a good listener is important to me. I often find myself telling people whatever I think will make them feel good. That's more important than absolutely being honest and telling K. to get a new haircut.

I went bike riding with A. and C. It was lots of fun. It bugs me that we always end up going wherever A. wants to go. I wanted to head to the ice cream parlor, but didn't speak up. I put off studying for my math test until almost 11 P.M. I kept falling asleep and didn't learn much. I don't know whether to practice formulas or study the chapter. I should have asked, should have taken better notes, and should have started studying earlier! Maybe I need to make a study schedule and stick to it. Otherwise, I'll never get into college.

EXERCISE

One way to understand your personal values is through self-assessment. Ask your guidance counselor to give you a values-clarification assessment. In the meantime, try taking the following values quiz.

For each item on the following pages, mark how important you think it is to you. If you're not sure, ask yourself, "Would I drive 200 miles for this (to go to church, visit a friend, vote)?"

	Very Important	Important	Somewhat Important	Unimportant
God				
Church				
Family				
Doing my best				
Friends				
Grades				
Being sensitive to the feelings of others				
Sports/ extracurricular activities				
School				
Independence				
Winning				
Economic security				
Inner peace				
Adventure				
Serving others				

	Very Important	Important	Somewhat Important	Unimportant
My country				
Status				
Respect from others				
Self-respect				
Fun				
Honesty				
Home				
Money				
Prestige				
Fame				
TV				
Dating				
Sex				
Possessions				
Hobbies				
Being included				
What others think of me				
The arts				
Popularity				
Health				
Compassion				
Excellence				
Love				

Evaluate those items you've indicated as very important. Ask yourself how many of your decisions and daily actions reflect your values. Do the same for the items you consider unimportant. How much do your values affect your lifestyle?

VALUE QUESTIONS

Another way to get at the root of your values is to ask yourself questions. Remember that the more you understand your own values, the better equipped you'll be to handle the tough choices in a new career.

Take a few minutes to answer these questions as honestly as you can:

- What are my dreams?
- Who are my mentors or idols?
- Of what things am I proudest:
  - about myself physically, mentally, emotionally?
  - in connection with my family?
  - at school?
  - a talent?
  - with my hands?
  - verbally?
  - something nobody knows but me?
- What do I want most out of life?

Complete the following:

- At least I'm somebody who . . .
- People disagree, but I think . . .
- Secretly, I wish . . .
- If I had one week to live, I'd . . .
- If I got a million dollars, I'd . . .

- Nobody can change my mind about . . .
- By the time I'm 65, I want to . . .
- Define yourself in four words: "I am _____, _____, _____, and _____."
- Define who you want to be in four words: "I wish I were _____, _____, _____, and _____."
- My personal motto could be:
- Three things I could never live without are: _____, _____, and _____.

Now examine your answers. Did you learn anything about yourself? Would your friends be surprised at any of your answers? Are you surprised by anything?

Know yourself and your values. They should form the basis for goals, decisions, and actions.

Most important to you above everything else are your integrity and personal values. You always can lose a job and get another one. You always can lose money and make more. But once you compromise your integrity and personal values, they can never be regained.

—Tom Ischgrund in *The Insider's Guide to the Top 20 Careers in Business and Management: What It's Really Like to Work in Advertising, Computers, Banking, Management, and Many More!*

ETHICS

Ethics deals with right and wrong. It's the code of unwritten rules that governs how we act toward others. In fact, "ethics" comes from the Greek word *ethos*, meaning "character." Socrates, the great fifth-

"Ethics" comes from the Greek word ethos, *meaning "character."*

SURF THE WEB: HELPFUL WEBSITES ABOUT VALUES AND ETHICS

Ethics Resource Center
http://www.ethics.org

Ethics Update
http://ethics.acusd.edu

Faith and Values.com
http://www.faithandvalues.com

Institute for American Values
http://www.americanvalues.org

Institute for Global Ethics
http://www.globalethics.org

Leader Values.com
http://www.leader-values.com

Legal Ethics.com
http://www.legalethics.com

century B.C. Greek philosopher, asked his students to ask themselves this question: "Why do you do what you do?"

Whereas values are the things we consider important, ethics are the "shoulds" and "should nots" of living we adhere to as we try to get what we want.

SHOULDS AND SHOULD NOTS

When Juanita's boss asked her to lie for him, Juanita experienced a personal ethical conflict. She wanted to succeed in her career. She wanted to please her boss. But somewhere inside her, she heard a voice telling her not to lie. Thus, she had an ethical dilemma.

Few of us will ever know exactly where we got all our ideas of moral "shoulds" and "should nots." Much of our ethical make up comes from our parents, families, peers, and religion or belief system.

Ethics and equity and the principles of justice do not change with the calendar.

—D. H. Lawrence, British author

Imagine yourself in these situations and think about what you would do.

You are part of a public-relations campaign designed to sell fast food. You know that your company's product isn't as healthy as your competitor's product. Yet you're expected to create slogans making false claims about your fast food's superiority. What would you do?

Christine found herself in this situation (though not over fast food). She values honesty and integrity, but she also values her own creativity . . . and her job. Her decision was to go all out on the campaign. She refrained from quoting false statistics or creating mythical testimonials. But she did make general claims—false claims—that her company's product lasts longer and is more popular than that of the competition. Although Christine wasn't 100-percent satisfied with her decision, she feels she made the best decision she could.

Other people have chosen to resign or have asked to be released from a campaign they didn't feel they could endorse. Think about ethical issues such as this now, so you won't be completely surprised later.

A customer comes to you with a complaint. You know her complaint is valid because you've heard it from many others this month. Company policy, however, is to deny wrongdoing because of the store's no-return policy. How will you handle this customer?

FACT

Ethics are a hot topic of debate in the United States today. Ethics Update.com lists case studies on hundreds of topics that currently make headlines, including:

Academic ethics

Affirmative action in college admissions

Business ethics

Equal Opportunity Harassment

Journalism ethics

Violence on television

Environmental ethics

Drilling in the Alaskan wilderness

Bioethics

Organ transplants

Designer babies

Social ethics

Nonsmoking facilities

Personal ethics

Lying on your resume

Legal ethics

Racial profiling

Travis and Sandra work for a company with a similar no-return policy. They've handled this situation in different ways, according to their individual ethical codes. Travis follows the company's advice to the letter. He believes what his boss does is up to him. Because of his personal ambition and loyalty to his boss, Travis never tells the customer that the product is probably defective.

Most of Sandra's personal ethics come from her faith. Since she can't reconcile the silent deceit of not being completely honest with the customer, Sandra often tells the customer that other products like hers have been returned, and she advises the customer not to purchase the same brand again. Sandra explained her decision to her boss, who agreed to let her handle customers this way as long as the company doesn't suffer from Sandra's honesty. Sandra says if she's told not to be honest, she's prepared to look for a new job.

FACT

When research associates at the Institute for American Values asked parents what their basic responsibility was, the number one answer was: "Teaching my kids right from wrong."

YOUR PERSONAL CODE OF ETHICS

Become familiar with your own already-existing code of ethics. Understanding your unwritten rules will help you make decisions you can live with.

Ask yourself the following questions.

Gossiping with friends is generally considered unethical workplace behavior. Develop your own code of ethics so you will know what behavior to avoid at work. (Corbis)

- Do you cheat on tests? What unwritten rules influence your decision?
- Would you try to date your best friend's steady? It's not illegal. So why would you or would you not do this?
- Would you smoke a cigarette if you were positive you wouldn't get caught? Virtue is going beyond what you're legally bound to do.
- Would you gossip about a friend? An acquaintance? An enemy? Does your answer change? Why?
- Would you tell a white lie to a teacher or parent if it saved you from a hassle?
- Would you tell a white lie if it saved someone's feelings?

Examine your decisions. See if you can decipher your own ethical code. Is it the way you want it to be? If not, now's the time to start changing it—before you hit the pressures of a new career.

EXERCISE

- If your house were on fire, what 10 items would you try to rescue?
- Write five bumper sticker slogans you wouldn't mind sticking on your car.
- Your corporation is secretly dumping toxic materials into the river that runs through your city. Will you do anything about it? If so, what? What values and ethics come into play in your decision?

IN SUMMARY . . .

- It is important to know what your values are so that you can easily make decisions.
- Observe yourself and keep a journal of your daily thoughts and actions. This will help you figure out what you value.
- Figure out what your personal code of ethics is so you don't get into uncomfortable situations at work.

3

BECOME MORE RELIABLE AND RESPONSIBLE

In one survey, employers were asked to name the one quality they look for more than any other in a would-be employee. More than 75 percent responded, "Dependability or responsibility." So if you want to make the "Most Wanted" list of career applicants, be the kind of person on whom others can depend.

FACT

According to Dr. Richard Swensen, author of *Margin: Restoring Emotional, Physical, Financial, and Time Reserves to Overloaded Lives,* you are more likely to be thought of as dependable if you aren't constantly losing things. The average American will spend one year of his/her life searching through desk clutter looking for misplaced objects.

The best way to prove you're dependable is through your actions. Showing up on time and completing assigned tasks are good examples of dependable behavior. If you don't come through on these basic responsibilities, you won't have your job very long.

BE ON TIME

Whether you're digging ditches or trading stocks, you'd better show up to work on time.

Whether you're digging ditches or trading stocks, you'd better show up to work on time. Chapter 7 discusses time management in detail. But for now, just know that if you're in the habit of running late, you'd better shake the habit.

Kelly could work an interview like nobody's business. While all her friends scrambled for jobs their last year of college, Kelly was offered every job she interviewed for. She had no trouble getting jobs. Keeping them was a different story.

Kelly, now a valued employee of Southwest Airlines, can laugh about the rude awakening of her first job—make that jobs. "I started as a trainee in an investment firm," Kelly says. "I'd always been late to my classes. So I thought I was doing great when I came in a couple of minutes late. But they yelled at me. I just thought my supervisor was mean. So I quit."

The same thing happened to Kelly at her next two jobs. When she landed the job at Southwest Airlines though, she was determined to keep it. "I set my alarm early. I left my apartment early enough to allow for traffic. I'd almost made the first six-month probation period. If you go six months without missing any time or being late, you get a free, reserved air ticket anywhere in the United States. With two weeks to go, my car broke down on the freeway. I was seven minutes late. I didn't get the ticket. But my habit of tardiness was over. I haven't been late in over a year."

SURF THE WEB: TIME MANAGEMENT

If you are organized, it is easier to be on time. For help with time management, visit the following websites:

Mind Tools.com
http://www.mindtools.com/page5.html

Organize Tips.com
http://www.organizetips.com

Organize Your World.com
http://wwww.organizeyourworld.com

Professional Organizers Web Ring
http://www.organizerswebring.com

FACT

According to a recent survey detailed in the *New York Times,* 70 percent of students confessed to academic tardiness.

HOW TO GET TO WORK ON TIME

- Set your alarm 30 minutes earlier.
- Always plan to get to work early—not on time.
- Use the buddy system with a punctual coworker.
- Have that second cup of coffee after you get to work.
- To avoid bad traffic hours, leave an hour early. Use the extra time to get work done, read, or eat breakfast.
- Iron and set out your clothes the night before.
- Keep your gas tank filled.
- Have a Plan B for emergencies—someone who can take you to work, or a cab to call if your car won't start.
- Never carpool with tardy people.
- Count on something going wrong and plan accordingly.

GETTING THE JOB DONE

Another basic responsibility is simply doing your job. Most jobs aren't like school. You don't put in your time from 8:00 A.M. to 3:00 P.M. and leave as soon as the bell rings. You don't slide by with minimum effort. At the very least, you hold up your end and get the job done.

Nancy thought of herself as a pretty hard worker when she joined the library staff at a city branch. During her first week, Nancy's boss gave her a list of duties. But instead of taking the list and getting those duties completed, Nancy kept seeing other jobs she could be doing. She wanted to recommend children's books for the library to purchase. She thought of a different way to arrange cassettes.

At the end of the week, Nancy was called into the head librarian's office. The library staff was

HOW TO GET THE JOB DONE

- **Do the part you dread first.**
- **Mentally move your actual deadline up a week.**
- **Make priority lists.**
- **Ask questions as soon as you get stuck.**

disappointed in Nancy's first-week performance. She hadn't been goofing off. But she failed to get the job done. After that, Nancy made sure she completed every item on her duty list every day. Although her ideas for improvement were useful, she realized she had to focus on her assigned duties first.

THE ART AND IMPORTANCE OF FOLLOW-THROUGH

When someone says, "I'll call you," do you expect a call? If somebody borrows your pen, what are the chances you'll get it back? How many times has a friend borrowed something (a book, a T-shirt) and forgotten to return it? When you call a store or business and ask them to return the call, do they?

The truth is that most people don't follow through on the "little things." You can't really count on what they say they'll do, even if you know their intention is good. But if you have a friend who does what he says he'll do, that's a friend you want to keep. That's the kind of a person you can depend on when you need help. If you become someone others can count on, someone who pays attention to the little things, you'll be a success no matter what career path you take.

Tara learned the art of follow-through as a child and put it to use when she was hired as a clerk in a medical clinic. Tara explains, "My mother was a stickler for making us do our chores. If I didn't feed the rabbit, I didn't get an after-school snack. If I told Grandma I'd call her, I'd better do it."

Then Tara was elected to her high school student council. "Before student council, I would have said the only important jobs went to the officers. But after working on committees, I realized it took all of us. They started giving me the jobs that had to get done. So when I started working at the clinic, I was willing to work hard at any job. And my bosses appreciated it. They almost seemed surprised when I'd follow through without anybody making me. Everybody there realizes how important the so-called little things are."

Because Tara proved faithful in the "little things," her bosses began handing over bigger responsibilities. Her follow-through skills earned her a place of leadership in the office.

You can quickly make an impression simply by saying you will do something, then doing it.

If you want to make yourself indispensable in your job, follow through with everything. In fact, you can quickly make an impression simply by saying you will do something, then doing it. If you know of a magazine article that might help your bosses or one of your team members, mention it one day and then bring a copy the next day. Be consistent.

Write down the little things in meetings. Someone says, "We need more copy paper." If you follow through and get the paper, people will recognize your initiative. Everybody complains because the office is out of coffee. You can be the only one who thinks of that little need and brings in coffee the next day. Prove how dependable you can be.

HOW TO EARN A REPUTATION AS SOMEONE TO COUNT ON

- **Get to work early. Beat your deadlines if you can.**
- **Stay after hours to get work done.**
- **Offer to show a relevant article to a coworker; deliver it the next day.**
- **Remember people's preferences (in food or color, for example) and use them when you have a chance.**
- **Return borrowed books quickly.**
- **If a coworker shows interest in your resource, give her a copy the next day.**
- **Be a detail-oriented person.**
- **Take great notes in meetings and refer to them when the meeting stalls.**
- **Do the little things nobody wants to do (phone calls, legwork, copying).**

Whoever can be trusted with very little can also be trusted with much.

—Luke 16:10

Al started working part time in a local Wal-Mart store when he was still in high school. He credits his rapid advancement to his follow-through with customers. Al says, "When a customer comes to me, he wants something. If I don't have exactly what he wants, I have two choices. I can say, 'We don't have it.' Or I can do all I can to follow through and help the customer."

One Christmas, Al drove 40 miles on his own time to get a toy that a customer wanted for her daughter. Then he called the customer until he reached her and arranged to meet her at her office so she'd have the gift in time.

You may not have to go quite that far. But you'll have more satisfied customers if you go the extra mile and follow through with your service.

PERSONAL RESPONSIBILITY

Dependability and responsibility begin at home. If you feel you haven't grown up yet, do it now. Take charge of yourself. Being responsible means keeping a clean living space and paying your bills on time. It means balancing your schedule so you get enough sleep and can perform well at your job.

You can become more responsible by doing the little things, such as laundry, dishes, and taking the garbage out, in a punctual manner. Building personal responsibility also means making much larger, more important commitments and following through with them.

FINANCIAL RESPONSIBILITY

Even if you get only a few bucks for a weekly allowance or earn eight dollars for babysitting each week, budget your money. Once you're out on your own, paying for rent, food, entertainment, and insurance, you'll have to keep a handle on your finances. If you don't, it will affect your work.

FACT

Here's how economists suggest allotting monthly income:

Housing, which can include mortgage or rent, utilities, insurance, taxes, and home maintenance: 35%

Transportation, which can include car payment, auto insurance, tag or license, gasoline, and parking: 15%

Savings, which should include three to six months of income saved for an emergency, at least 10%

Debt, which can include student loans, credit card debts, and medical debts: 15%

Other, which includes food, clothing, entertainment, medical expenses, and vacations: 25%

Source: Consumer Credit Counseling Service (http://www.cccssf.org)

Start a simple log to record your spending. Once you see where your money (or your parents' money) is going, you'll know the areas you need to budget. How much can you afford to spend in each area monthly?

One tip is to mark a set of envelopes with the financial category you're budgeting. For example, if you live with your parents, you may need only a few envelopes: Car, Entertainment, Clothes, Gifts, CDs, Savings, and Miscellaneous. Until you get the hang of budgeting, put the actual money allotted into each envelope. When the money's gone, you're done. This might keep you from spending everything on movies, for example.

Whatever your system, get a head start on handling your finances. It will be one less worry when you start your career.

PRIVATE RESPONSIBILITY

Another part of your personal responsibility will be keeping your personal life in order. Don't bring your romantic, family, or friendship dramas to the office.

Try to live a well-balanced life. Do you have a hobby, something to take your mind off work? Are you in the habit of exercising regularly and eating right? The more lifestyle areas you can get in control now, the better.

TEAM RESPONSIBILITY

Once you become part of a working team, your responsibilities take on an added dimension. You have to become a team player. Each person on a team needs to take personal responsibility for team relationships. You'll have to do more than just be a nice guy. You have to take responsibility for your team's development.

What does it mean to be responsible for team relationships? First, avoid team conflicts. Work for a consensus. Do what you can to draw out quieter team members, to smooth over personality conflicts. Respect and value the members of your team.

When you become part of a team, your responsibilities shift. The team's success becomes more important than your personal success. For example, what would you do if your team voted on Plan B, but you knew beyond a shadow of a doubt that Plan A was better? What if your team met the entire department to discuss Plan B, and the company boss asked you for your opinion? Where does your responsibility lie? Would you:

1. Use the opportunity to get your team to change their minds?
2. Tell your boss Plan B isn't your idea?
3. Explain why you believe A is a better plan?
4. Keep your mouth shut?
5. Discuss one or two points you can agree on in Plan B?

Most professionals with team experience would say 5 is the right answer. As a team player, your first responsibility is to your teammates. Express your opinions tactfully and fully in team meetings. But once your team decides on a plan of action, that plan becomes your plan. When the team meeting ends and Plan B is adopted, your responsibility is to help your team with that plan.

As a team player, your first responsibility is to your teammates.

PERSONAL INITIATIVE

One of your responsibilities will be to act on your own initiative. Don't always wait until someone tells you what to do. Ask for advice. Learn from people with experience and expertise. But don't distrust your own abilities. Have the confidence to act on your own and to follow through, without bothering your boss with every little problem.

You run an element of risk when you act on your own. But risk isn't necessarily bad. Few successes come without some element of risk. Do your homework and research. Don't be afraid to act.

DOS AND DON'TS OF WORKING WITH A TEAM

Do	Don't
Remember that your first responsibility is to the team.	Be selfish.
Make an effort to speak up and draw out quiet members.	Keep to yourself.
Be honest with all team members.	Do anything to jeopardize the team's success.
Monitor the team's progress.	Assume someone else is responsible for a task.
Be fair and work your hardest.	Try to cheat others by being lazy.
Listen to your boss' orders and requests.	Try to do things your way only.

If you make a mistake, there's one more opportunity to exercise your responsibility. Admit your mistake. Apologize. Don't try to rationalize or excuse your error. Take responsibility and say you're sorry. Then do whatever it takes to try to make up for it.

One general manager, looking back over his career, said, "I've made a lot of mistakes. But in the long run, the mistake itself didn't matter much. It was the way I handled the mistake. That's what made an impression."

Being responsible and dependable is what most employers value more highly than anything else. And it's a quality that's within your grasp. Go for it!

IN SUMMARY . . .

- If you want others to regard you as reliable and responsible, the first step is to get to work on time.
- Volunteer to do projects that others don't want—this is the way to move up the ladder and eventually obtain more responsibility.
- To be considered reliable, there are many responsibilities you must meet, including financial, team, and personal commitments.

EXERCISE

- Name five less-than-responsible things you did last week. Beside each, write what you might have done differently.
- Draw a pie chart showing how you spend your money. Next, draw a pie chart showing how you'd like to start spending your money. Then draw up a budget that reflects the second pie chart.
- Pick one person to convince that you are highly dependable. List 10 "little things" you can do over the next month to prove your point.

- In order to get the job done, start with the task you dread the most and mentally move your deadline up one week. Make priority lists and ask questions throughout the project to ensure that it is completed successfully.
- To gain a reputation as someone others can count on, always beat your deadline, return borrowed objects promptly, and be detail oriented.

4

PROFESSIONAL EXCELLENCE

What if you got a 99 percent on a science test? You'd probably feel pretty good about yourself. Or say you get 95 percent on your history midterm. You'll take it, right?

While 99 percent or even 95 percent is usually great on school exams, in the business world it just won't do. In business you must strive for excellence—100 percent—at all times. Here's what would happen if the following businesses and agencies settled for 99 percent instead of 100:

- The IRS would not have collected tax forms from 1,312,480 individuals in 2002.
- Every month, 515 planes landing at O'Hare International Airport in Chicago would crash.
- About $129,000 would be spent this year on CDs that won't play.
- The *Oxford English Dictionary* would contain 2,311 misspelled entries.

When you start your career, you raise your personal stakes. Always strive for excellence on the job.

FACT

Office Team, a company that provides businesses with temporary workers, asked some of the nation's largest companies, "How many typos in a resume does it take for you to decide not to consider a candidate?" Their response: Forty-five percent said one typo was enough to eliminate the candidate; thirty-one percent said two typos and you're out.

ESTABLISHING A WORK ETHIC

Excellence isn't an abstract prize that only a chosen few can win. Excellence is almost always within your power—if you're willing to work for it. You can always work harder and longer. Unlike in school, the bell doesn't dismiss you from the workplace.

Marcia recalls what it was like for her to attend her 10-year high school reunion. Although in high school no one ever noticed her, at the reunion she was a hit—confident and successful.

"I always felt I worked twice as hard for good grades as everybody else had to," Marcia explains.

SEVEN WAYS TO TELL YOU'RE NOT WORKING HARD ENOUGH

1. Your boss calls you lazy.
2. Your coworkers never want to be assigned to projects you're working on.
3. You're bored at the office.
4. You've developed into an excellent Solitaire player on your office computer.
5. Your wastebasket is empty.
6. You never need new office supplies.
7. You're fired.

"But I'm glad now. It made me a hard worker on the job. My bosses appreciated how hard I worked. And now I'm the boss!"

The work ethic and identifying ourselves with work and through work is not only alive and well but more present now than at any time in history.

—John Gillis, historian, Rutgers University

There's a particular pride and satisfaction you get from working hard. You've probably experienced it somewhere—training for an athletic competition, studying extra for a final, finishing an art project after hours of labor.

A young man named Popescu came from Romania and took the only job he could get: bagging groceries in a Midwest supermarket. For a couple of years, he worked as hard as he could at his job. In 1996, Popescu won a grocery-bagger competition, qualifying for National Bag-Off, the National Grocers Association's best-bagger contest.

At the competition, the young Romanian was asked by a reporter, "Why do you work so hard at one of the company's lowest-paid positions?"

Popescu grinned and answered, "I'm here to work. What else should I do?" Later, when Popescu was promoted to day stocker, he worked even harder. "When you are raised to a higher position you want to do a better job," he explained. "You want them to think it was right that they put you in that position."

UNSELFISH EXCELLENCE

Hard work and excellence do more than make you look good. You can transform your work team with your professional attitude of unselfish excellence.

Amanda works for a small environmental agency in the Northwest. But she claims she learned the rewards of unselfish excellence in her high school choir. Amanda was usually the soloist for concerts and performances. But in choir, she picked up a valuable lesson. No matter how hard Amanda practiced her solo, the whole choir had to come together. Otherwise, there would be no music—only noise.

Lack of will power has caused more failure than lack of intelligence or ability.

—Flower A. Newhouse, American author

Amanda's choir director encouraged small group rehearsals. Choir students learned each other's parts. Amanda helped other sopranos in every way she could. Instead of spending more time on her own part, spending time with her team paid better returns. She opted for team excellence. Their choir achieved beautiful music together and placed first in district competition.

"So that's what I started doing at work," Amanda said. "I looked for ways to help them. And I asked them for help, too. The whole team grew stronger. And I came to appreciate how much everyone else knew." Amanda learned the value of unselfish excellence.

PROFESSIONAL DRESS

Excellence involves more than just hard work. You need to conduct yourself as a professional in the way you dress, talk, and act.

For example, what should you wear to work? Your best bet is to ask and observe. Save your "fashion rebel" streak for after hours with your friends. At work, dress like a professional. This may mean different things in different work environments, but the safest route is always to dress conservatively.

DOS AND DON'TS OF PROFESSIONAL DRESS

Do	Don't
Wear conservative clothes.	Be flashy.
Wear a conservative hairstyle.	Wear hair too long.
Look crisp.	Look rumpled.
Wear dress shoes.	Wear sneakers.
Use deodorant/antiperspirant.	Douse yourself with scent.
Use makeup sparingly.	Use evening makeup.
Limit your jewelry.	Wear too many earrings or rings.
Cover up any tattoos you may have.	Have tattoos on display.

If you want the job, you have to look the part. If you want the promotion, you have to look promotable. If you want respect, you have to dress as well or better than the industry standard.

—Susan Bixler in *Professional Presence: The Total Program for Gaining That Extra Edge in Business by America's Top Corporate Image Consultant*

Imagine walking into your first job. You get only one shot at a first impression. What they see is what they'll think they got. Try not to be the most or least dressy person in the office. Business attire usually means suits for men and suits, dresses, or skirts for women. That's a good place to start. You can always adapt and dress more casually later if you need to.

Don't let anything get in the way of people's discovering how much you have to offer.

Don't forget the basics—neat, clean, and good personal hygiene. The underlying principle of all this is: Don't let anything get in the way of people's discovering how much you have to offer.

PROFESSIONAL ETIQUETTE

Professional etiquette includes everything from good table manners and environmental awareness to introductions and the infamous office holiday party.

It is important to learn the proper etiquette for business lunches. This man is inappropriately chatting about personal matters on his cell phone in the middle of an important business lunch. (Index Stock Imagery)

Etiquette is a set of rules we live by. Manners are the way we put those rules into effect.

Mind Your Manners

If you don't think manners count in the professional world, listen to Rick's story.

"I joined a production team and felt pretty good about my skills and abilities. My first day, the manager took us out to eat at a fancy restaurant. All of a

TIPS FOR OFFICE LUNCHEONS

- Don't order "hand food" (fried chicken, ribs) or overly messy food (spaghetti).
- Put your napkin on your lap.
- Don't order alcohol.
- Don't order first.
- Chew with your mouth closed.
- Take small bites.
- Don't talk with your mouth full.
- When more than one fork is at your place setting, start with the outside one and work your way in.
- Don't blow your nose at the table.
- Don't rush through your meal.

sudden I felt like a tagalong kid. I didn't know which fork to use. I ordered spareribs, then felt like a cave dweller eating with my hands. I ordered first and got a beer. Nobody else ordered alcohol. I wished I'd listened when my mom used to yell stuff at me during dinner—like 'napkin on lap' and stuff. It was a nightmare."

Practice good table manners. It's part of being a professional. Be safe when you eat with your coworkers.

Don't order anything that will be messy to eat, such as fried chicken, ribs, and spaghetti. Don't order alcohol. Follow other people's leads and don't get the most expensive thing on the menu. And by all means—don't slurp your soup.

Greetings

It may sound silly, but don't forget to smile. Everyone in your office deserves a smile and a simple, friendly greeting from you. Remember names and titles, too.

An account manager offers a friendly greeting to her new coworker. (Corbis)

Learn how to introduce people properly. For example, say you are introducing your client, Dr. Zhivago, to your coworker, Max Brown. Dr. Zhivago is the one you want to give more respect to, and he's the odd-one out, the stranger. Say his name first, and give him the information first:

"Dr. Zhivago, I'd like you to meet our accountant, Max Brown. Max, this is Dr. Zhivago, the client I told you about."

It's also a good idea to drop a conversation-starting piece of information to your coworker, such as: "Max, Dr. Zhivago used to live in your neck of the woods, Boston." Then your coworker can take it from there.

When you're introduced to someone, stand up (if you weren't already doing so). If you are busy with a project, put it aside and give your full attention to the introduction, rather than appearing preoccupied. Extend your hand to give a handshake and a friendly greeting. Be sure to use a firm, confident grip when you shake someone's hand—some people believe that a weak or lazy handshake is a sign that you're not a tough businessperson.

FACT

Employees of one construction company attended a seminar on business etiquette to learn, among other things, how to talk to clients on the phone. The chief financial officer reported: "Clients want to hear a smile in your voice. Showing consideration for and an interest in the caller are the keys to telephone courtesy."

Environmental Awareness

Most modern offices have taken part in the environmental awareness movement. If you're wasteful, it won't go unnoticed. Look for a place to recycle your cans and paper. To cut down on paper cups, bring in your own mug. Try not to waste paper. Look for ways to cut corners, to reuse, to recycle.

Unspoken After-Hours Etiquette

When office hours officially end, your professionalism should not. The happily drunk office worker who dances half-naked with a lamp shade on his head at the office Christmas party may make a funny scene in an old movie, but it's not professional.

Most work teams are close enough that what happens outside the office has a way of finding its way into the office. Few secrets survive. As one wise person put it, "Don't do anything you wouldn't want reported in tomorrow morning's newspaper."

FACT

More than 75 percent of workers surveyed had attended a happy hour together, and more than 45 percent had dined or gone out with coworkers on weekends, according to a recent survey by the At-A-Glance Group.

PROFESSIONAL ATTITUDE

It's difficult to define, but there's a certain attitude that professionals must maintain at work. This attitude includes the way you act toward coworkers, the expectations you have at work, what you talk about or bring with you to work, and the way you carry yourself on the job.

At home or in high school, you may have grown accustomed to frequent praise as a means of encouragement. Your teacher praised you for working hard, and your mom applauded a good grade. But don't expect that kind of hand-holding from your boss or coworkers—they're too busy. Do your job correctly and be professional.

Keep an even tone about yourself. Even when the pace gets hectic and anxieties run high in the office, tell yourself, "No drama at work." Speak calmly and not too loudly. Take deep breaths, and wait before you react and get pulled into a frenzy. Earn a reputation as someone with a level head.

PROFESSIONAL PRIVACY

Possibly the best advice on professionalism comes from Lin: "Keep your private life private . . . and leave your love life at home where it belongs!" After a year working for a Dallas investment firm, Lin learned the hard way how important it was to guard her privacy. "I was going through a break up. Every day I'd come in and spill my heart out. My coworkers listened, but after a while, I felt like nobody took my work seriously. They felt sorry for me and didn't give me a chance at big accounts."

Sharon, on the other hand, is determined not to date anyone from the office and to keep her private life private. When she's at her job in the food industry, she guards her personal privacy. During her first six months at her new job, Sharon broke up with her boyfriend. But she never unloaded her emotions at the office.

Sharon says, "I learned in high school that there were certain girls—and guys—who dump everything. Their love lives were the only things that mattered to them. If they broke up with a boyfriend, you'd see them crying in the halls or running out of class in tears. I would have loved to talk it out with the people I work with. But I didn't want to be one of those girls like I knew in high school. So I went to work. I did my job. Then I went home and cried my eyes out on my own time."

PROFESSIONAL HONESTY

You can't attain professional excellence without basic honesty. Do you consider yourself an honest person? Most of us do. But your level of professional honesty and integrity has to be high. You have to remain above reproach at all times.

SURF THE WEB: WORK ETHICS

Rethinking Work
http://www.worklifebook.org

The Work Ethic Site
http://www.coe.uga.edu/~rhill/workethic/

Work Ethic Wizard
http://www.workethicwizard.com

CUSTOMER HONESTY

Another place for honesty is in your customer relationships. You may be able to push a sale by stretching the claims of your product, but you'll probably lose in the long run. The customer will eventually find out the truth, and you will have lost all the sales he might have brought back. Always go out of your way to play fair, even in the tightest negotiations.

COMPANY LOYALTIES

You owe loyalty and honesty to your company, too. J. R. Richmond managed Sears and J. C. Penney stores before owning his own department store. He says, "The first thing I demand in an employee is honesty.

TIPS FOR FAIR PLAY WITH CLIENTS

- Always be up-front. If you don't know, say so.
- Don't twist words. Don't say "challenge," if you mean "problem."
- Keep your word. Return calls, and do what you say you will.
- Treat each client as an important individual.
- Don't make excuses. Take responsibility for errors.

I had one clerk who charged full for sale items and pocketed the difference. Another I caught in a scam. He'd fill a suitcase with our store items. Then his wife or brother or somebody would come in, and he'd sell them the suitcase."

FACT

According to the Fireman's Fund Insurance Company, at least $67 billion is lost each year in the United States to employee cheating and stealing.

Everybody's dishonest gain is somebody's loss. Strive for professional excellence and integrity. Honesty is still the best policy.

DISHONEST BEHAVIORS TO AVOID AT WORK

- Stealing company materials
- Punching out at the wrong time
- Calling in sick when you're not
- Tending to personal matters or projects instead of doing work
- Making numerous personal long-distance calls on company time
- Taking credit for someone else's idea
- Lying on your expense account
- Saying you did work when you didn't

IN SUMMARY . . .

- To maintain professional excellence, you must have the right attitude, honesty, and appropriate business etiquette.
- Always keep your private life separate from your work life.
- To be considered professional, dress conservatively and have a neat, clean appearance.

EXERCISE

- Be honest. Name three dishonest things you've done in the past six months. How did you rationalize your dishonesty?
- Try formally introducing two people this week.
- Have a quasi-formal dinner during which you try your best to have perfect manners.
- Plan your wardrobe for the first five days of a new job.

- Everyone in your office deserves a smile and a friendly greeting. Try to remember names and titles, too.
- When you are at a business lunch or dinner, be very conscious of your table manners, do not order first, and do not order alcohol.
- Maintain a reputation as a responsible professional even after-hours with coworkers.
- Be fair and follow a strong work ethic at all times; if you try to cut corners, you're cheating yourself, your coworkers, and your employer.

5

BE AGGRESSIVELY NICE

Dian and three of her friends graduated from the same business school. Dian knew two of those friends had better skills than she did. Yet after three years, she was the only one securely on a successful career path. Since they had all worked hard and tried the same businesses, her success remained a mystery to Dian until her boss invited her to lunch.

Dian relates the conversation that gave her insight into her own success. "We finished discussing assignments, and my boss said: 'Dian, you have what it takes to make it.' I asked her what she meant. She said, 'You are *aggressively nice*. Nice won't get it, and neither will aggression. But together, that's a lethal combination.'

"That changed the way I look at myself," Dian continues. "Even in high school on committees, I'd practiced what this woman was telling me. When I was pushy, nobody listened to me. And when I was too nice, nobody paid attention. But aggressively nice worked."

Being aggressively nice means being thoughtful and considerate while following through with thoughtfulness. In order to develop personally and professionally, you must be kind and mindful of others in a way that is not seen as overbearing.

PUT YOUR THOUGHTFULNESS IN WRITING

Kim says she comes by her thoughtfulness honestly. "My mother would sit us down at the kitchen table the day after Christmas. And she wouldn't let us up until we'd written every last thank-you note."

FACT

Franklin D. Roosevelt wrote personal thank-you notes to mechanics and acquaintances. He remembered their names and said one of the most important ways of gaining goodwill was by making people feel important. Maybe that's why he was elected president four times.

Kim's habit ended up getting her one of her first jobs. "I had my first book accepted for publication by Prentice-Hall. I was so excited, until my manuscript came back from the editor. Every line had a correction or suggestion." But instead of despairing, Kim studied each mark until she understood why it read better their way.

"When I was done, I felt I'd had the best editing course in the world. I'd learned so much! So I wrote the editor and told her so. I thanked her. She wrote me back that in her 20 years as an editor, nobody had ever written her a thank-you for editing. When my book was done, that editor offered me a job as a reader for her. Eventually, I did freelance editing for them." Kim's thoughtfulness paid off. If she'd remained silently

WAYS TO BE AGGRESSIVELY NICE IN THE OFFICE

Instead of . . .	Try . . .
blasting your radio loudly and disturbing others	playing it softly on a station that everyone agrees on
eating by yourself every day	encouraging coworkers to eat together
claiming the easiest projects for yourself	offering to do some of the less-desired projects occasionally to be fair
arriving at work silently and with your head down	greeting all of your coworkers with a smile and "hello"
being mentally grateful to a helpful coworker	letting coworkers know you appreciate their help through a thank-you note or email

grateful, that editor never would have known. And Kim wouldn't have gotten a job out of the deal.

MENTORS AND MAILROOMS

It's not just the boss's impression of you that counts. Be nice to every person you meet. Don't turn off the charm as soon as your boss leaves the room.

Brent works for a city transportation agency in the South. He admits he had to learn the hard way to be nice to everybody. "When I needed something from the mail room, for example, I called down and barked commands. If it didn't get to me fast enough, pity the guy who brought it. Before long, I noticed something odd. I was the last person to get anything from the mailroom. I learned my lesson."

Kris Bliss, a public-relations specialist in Los Angeles, says, "The first person you want to make friends with is the secretary. Nobody has more power or can help you more where it counts. These are people you want to have on your side. And always be friends with the mailroom. They know everything."

A great man shows his greatness by the way he treats little men.

—Thomas Carlyle, British historian

When someone at work does you a favor, say thanks. If a secretary goes out of the way to help you meet your deadline, write a thank-you note. For the receptionist who knows just how to handle those difficult calls, tell him what a great job you think he's doing. Show your appreciation.

Sometimes other people can fill in our blind spots. Trevor never considered himself hard to get to know. But in his senior year in high school he overheard a classmate refer to him as a snob. Trevor didn't feel like a snob, but for the next year he worked on the actions that may have made that impression. He smiled more, initiated conversations, and made sure he made eye contact when others spoke to him. He tried to show his interest in other people. He was learning to be aggressively nice.

IMPROVE INTERPERSONAL SKILLS IN THE OFFICE

Make a list of 10 ways you would like to be treated by team members. Use those principles to help you deal with others. Use the statements that follow as a guide in developing your list.

- I'd like to be respected.
- I'd like someone to listen when I talk.

EXERCISE

How nice are you? Circle the number that most fits the way you see yourself. Then ask at least four other people to fill out the assessment as they see you. Include a friend who knows you well, a family member, a teacher, and someone who barely knows you. How do the different views of you (yours and theirs) compare? How well do you know yourself? Do others perceive you as nice as you believe yourself to be?

	Always	Never	Sometimes	Usually
I smile a lot.	1	2	3	4
I'm friendly to all.	1	2	3	4
I converse easily with peers.	1	2	3	4
I converse easily with elders.	1	2	3	4
I contribute to discussions.	1	2	3	4
I'm easy to talk to.	1	2	3	4
I'm interested in others.	1	2	3	4
I'm respectful.	1	2	3	4
I'm generous.	1	2	3	4
I do my share of the work.	1	2	3	4
I'm dependable.	1	2	3	4
I'm honest.	1	2	3	4
I'm unselfish.	1	2	3	4
I'm polite and courteous.	1	2	3	4
I cooperate with others.	1	2	3	4
I'm an encourager.	1	2	3	4
I return phone calls.	1	2	3	4

- I'd like people to give me the benefit of the doubt.
- I'd like to be appreciated.
- I'd like to be given a chance to show what I can do.
- I'd like to be forgiven when I mess up and not have it constantly thrown in my face.
- I'd like to be congratulated when I do a good job.
- I'd like to be able to trust other people to do what they say they will do.
- I'd like to be left alone when I'm working on a deadline.
- I'd like others to ask me for my opinion.

BE AGGRESSIVELY NICE IN BUSINESS DEALINGS

What about when you're in the heat of a hostile deal with your competition? What if you're bidding against a competitor or trying to get the lowest price you can get out of your supplier? In times like those, how can a professional still be nice?

Goodwill is the one and only asset that competition cannot undersell or destroy.

—Marshall Field, American merchant

Sam Walton created a multimillion-dollar enterprise without losing his friendliness. An officer of one firm that did business with Wal-Mart remarked: "These people [Wal-Mart buyers] are as folksy and down-to-earth as homegrown tomatoes. But when you start dealing with them—when you get past that 'down home in Bentonville' business—they're as hard as nails and every bit as sharp. They'll drive as hard a deal as anyone anywhere."

You don't have to get nasty to make the best deal. Niceness works from a business standpoint. Read mission statements of major corporations. Often, their statements of purpose are ethically and morally oriented, encouraging employees to foster goodwill and help their communities.

The oldest business adage is, "The customer is always right."

Never forget that customers are real people, with needs and families and real frustrations. The oldest business adage is, "The customer is always right." Treat even surly customers with respect and try to help them solve their problems. Do your best to understand and empathize with each individual. Smile, greet, and remember names. People deserve to hear more than, "Next."

ARE YOU ASSERTIVE IN THE WORKPLACE?

In order to be heard and understood at work, you must be assertive in business dealings. If you can answer "yes" to most of the following situations, you are on the right track:

- I can make my own decisions and feel good about them.
- When I need help or a favor from a friend, I can ask directly for what I want rather than using indirect means like hinting.
- When someone does something that bothers me, I am able to express my feelings.
- I can make the first move toward beginning a friendship with someone I am getting to know.
- I can maintain my point of view in the face of a disagreement from an aggressive, opinionated person.
- I can stand up for my rights when someone in authority is rude or unreasonable.
- I am able to negotiate salary increases and changes in job title or function.

Source: Seneca College of Applied Arts and Technology

Sam Walton kept notoriously poor paperwork when he worked the floor in his stores. It's said he just couldn't stand to keep a customer waiting in line while he finished writing down a sale.

YOUR ROLE WITH YOUR TEAM

Even though you're the new kid on the team, you may be able to play a valuable role in defusing team conflicts. You can be nice to everybody.

But you can take it further—be aggressively nice on your work team. You start out unbiased, free from age-old resentments. Use your position as peacemaker. You won't like everybody on your team, and that's okay. Some of them may drive you crazy, but you may drive some of them crazy, too. Your teammates don't need to become your buddies, but respect everybody. Practice empathy. Let people vent around you, without your joining in. You don't have to fix things; you just have to try to understand them.

You'll be in better shape to be aggressively nice at the office if you meet all the personal needs you can outside the office. Come to work ready to work. Don't lug around a list of needs you expect your teammates to fulfill.

And no matter how nice you are, sooner or later, you'll run into conflict. It may be a personality conflict or a clash of wills. When it happens, be prepared to do whatever it takes to restore harmony. One of the best ways to be aggressively nice in the heat of battle is to apologize.

Never underestimate the power of an apology. You'll be amazed how far the words "I'm sorry" can take you. Many explosive situations are defused with this formula: Swallow, take a deep breath, and then say, "You're right. I'm wrong. Sorry." It takes a strong person to admit he was wrong.

Never underestimate the power of an apology.

In most conflicts, both parties are somewhat at fault. Even if the other guy was guiltier than you, you can still find something to apologize for. And your apology may be all that's needed to restore the peace. Be a peacemaker.

When in doubt, be nice—aggressively nice.

EXERCISE

- **Make up your own definition of what it means to be "aggressively nice."**
- **List three actions you could take today to express your gratitude to someone. Follow through with those actions.**
- **When was the last time you apologized to someone or someone apologized to you? What was the effect of the apology?**

It doesn't matter to me if a man is from Harvard or Sing Sing. We hire the man, not his history.

—Henry Ford, American industrialist and founder of Ford Motor Company

IN SUMMARY . . .

- Be kind to others in the workplace. Do aggressively nice things such as writing thank-you notes.
- Cooperate with your teammates and don't be afraid to apologize. You won't like every person on your team, but you do have to get along with each person.
- You can get amazing results without being nasty—niceness often works wonders in the business world.
- Let others know that you appreciate their work. This includes everyone from the secretary to your boss to the mailroom workers.

6

BE A LEARNER

Did you know that 89 percent of work knowledge is acquired on the job? No wonder many employers believe the number one responsibility of new workers is to become learners.

THE POWER OF QUESTIONS

Michael says he owes his relatively smooth transition to his first job to his high school literature teacher. "My teacher made us ask questions. We'd read a story that none of us understood, and he'd make us ask questions until we felt like we knew that story."

Michael took his bag of questions with him and used it from day one when he joined an administrative staff. "I just kept asking questions until I knew my duties and the ins and outs of the company."

Asking questions helps you get answers that equip you to do your job. So don't be afraid of looking or sounding stupid. It's better to be honest about your ignorance than to pretend you know more than you do; sooner or later, you'll be found out.

One of the most important business skills, particularly in the first few years of entering the real workplace, is the willingness to ask questions and learn as much as possible. There truly is no such thing as a dumb question! Many of the people I started with at my company are mid-level and senior executives because they asked questions of everybody.

—Ann Wolford, problem-solving expert

If you develop the habit of asking lots of questions while you are in school, you will continue this helpful practice in the workplace. (Corbis)

Fran really wanted to make a good impression her first day at work, since her cousin had gone out of his way to get her a job as a typist. But when the supervisor showed Fran where she'd work, Fran realized she'd be doing a lot more than typing.

Fran says, "She asked me if I knew WordPerfect. Before I knew what I was saying, I'd said 'yes.' Then I had to stare at the screen all day because I didn't have a clue. The next day, I had to tell the supervisor the truth. I felt about six inches tall crawling into her office."

It is important to be totally honest about how much you know from the start at a new job. Your employer doesn't expect you to know everything, so be honest about what you really do and don't know. To save yourself time and embarrassment, ask these key questions.

- How exactly does this work?
- Am I doing this satisfactorily?
- What could I do to do a better job?
- May I see if I understand you correctly?
- Is there someone I can go to if I need help?
- How could I help with that?
- Would you run that by me again?

Besides helping you learn your job, asking questions can get you a reputation as a learner—and that's a reputation you want. There's a world of difference between "I don't know" and "I'd like to know." Don't stop with your lack of knowledge. Make it clear that you really want to know how things work. You want to know all you can about this company. You just can't get enough.

Questions can help you handle conflicts and authority. Put your disagreements in the form of questions. "Do you think it would work to try this?" "What do you think about . . . ?" "If we tried this instead, what do you think might happen?"

Never underestimate the power of a good question.

Learning is not attained by chance. It must be sought for with ardor and attended to with diligence.

—Abigail Adams, wife of U.S. President John Adams

ROOKIE-YEAR LEARNER

Every employee should try to learn as much as possible. But as the new kid in your rookie year on the job, your role as a learner is different; as a rookie, you probably have to more to learn than everyone else, regardless of your experience.

When Ben joined a group of agricultural extension workers, he brought with him five years of technical education and notebooks full of the latest ideas. His work team had undertaken a county extension project that involved service to farming communities in Iowa. Ben read the plan and knew instantly he had a better idea.

Ben could hardly wait for the first project meeting. As soon as the team leader began reviewing objectives and asking for reports, Ben shared his idea. Instead of the enthusiasm and approval he had expected, Ben's revolutionary plan stirred no interest at all. After the meeting, Ben knew he had done something wrong. He just didn't know what.

Ben forgot his first duty to his work team—to learn. If one of the other members had suggested Ben's plan, it may have received a closer look, but maybe not. Maybe the team had already tried Ben's approach. But Ben was new. The others felt he still had a lot to learn.

SURF THE WEB: HOW TO ACT AND PERFORM AT WORK

Business-Person.com
http://www.business-person.com/etiquette/OfficeEtiquette.html

Gradview.com
http://www.gradview.com/careers/etiquette.html

Ravenworks.com
http://www.ravenwerks.com/practices/etiquette.htm

LEARNING THE ROPES

Your first year is a learning period in which you should strive to master your job. Learn all you can about your company and team members. Some companies appoint a mentor for each new employee. A mentor is a more experienced employee who will show you the ropes. Whether or not your company follows this practice, start looking for your own men-

RULES OF THE CUBE

As you get to know your new coworkers, there are a few rules to keep in mind if you are new to the "cubicle lifestyle."

- Don't just barge into someone's cubicle—wait to be invited in or knock if it's a tall cube.
- Avoid using the speakerphone.
- Be aware of how your voice carries.
- Avoid discussing private matters in your cubicle.
- Make a good impression by keeping your desk clean.

Sources: *The Cubicle Lifestyle,* ABCNews.com; *Business Etiquette* by Ann Marie Sabath

Two financial analysts collaborate on a project at a cubicle. If you work in a cubicle, it is important to work quietly and respect your coworkers' desires. (Corbis)

tor. (He or she may or may not be the mentor you're assigned.) Find someone whom you can ask anything. Make sure he or she is somebody who likes to answer questions. Be sensitive about taking up someone else's time. Since we tend to become like the people we spend time with, choose your mentor carefully, if you have a choice.

Also during your first year, learn as much as you can about other people's jobs. When you act interested, people consider you interesting. Besides that, you'll be better equipped to help your team if you have a good knowledge of your team members' responsibilities; you can pinch-hit when necessary.

EARN YOUR STRIPES

You may think that because you've been hired, you're automatically entitled to the same respect and consideration as everybody else. But when you start a job, you have to prove yourself and earn the respect of your team. While you're learning the business your first year, you're laying the foundation for your reputation.

What can you do to earn your stripes? Here are some answers given by team members, from postal workers and department store clerks to business managers and telemarketers.

- Work harder than anybody else. Come in early and leave late, even if all you do is polish your desk. Do more than you're asked to do. Develop a reputation as a hard worker.
- Have a positive attitude at the office, even if you feel you've made the worst mistake in

your life taking this job. Give coworkers a smile and a warm hello.

- Keep a notebook. Remember dates, names, clients, and instructions. Go home and memorize.
- Be a professional cheerleader, quick to congratulate (sincerely) and express appreciation.
- Be the most available person on your team. You will probably have more time than established team members. If you get a free minute, ask somebody what you can do to help. The best thing you have to offer your team is you—your time, your abilities, your energy.
- Stay sharp, ready for your big moment. When you first start at a job, your main responsibilities may be small, so do everything you can to learn about the company and help and encourage others. When you finally get the chance to do more, your research and observations of coworkers will be useful, and others will encourage you.
- Demonstrate your commitment to the company. Learn all you can about functions, titles, and clients. Ask others for

You have to prove yourself and earn the respect of your team.

their ideas about the future of the business. Do outside research and keep up on competitors. Be knowledgeable. Volunteer for assignments. Ask to sit in on meetings. Join professional organizations. Learn all you can.

TOP RESPONSIBILITIES FOR A LEARNER

- Ask questions.
- Learn your job.
- Learn the jobs of others on your team.
- Be a cheerleader for your team.
- Learn all you can about your company.
- Develop good relationships.
- Work hard.
- Be available to help where needed.
- Have a positive attitude.
- Volunteer for duties.
- Follow through on every responsibility.

HUMILITY—AN ACCURATE VIEW OF SELF

Good learners have discovered the secret of humility. Humility isn't thinking you're lowly and worthless. Humility means having an accurate, balanced picture of yourself that is neither too lofty nor too low.

FACT

A major telephone company conducted a study of 500 phone conversations to find out the most frequently used word. "I" won—it was spoken over 3,900 times.

Pride, pretentiousness, and power trips are behavioral dead-ends in the workplace. The path to good self-esteem isn't to kid yourself about yourself. Know yourself well, and accept yourself. That's healthy. Not knowing everything is not the end of the world. You can learn what you don't know now.

Don't forget your role as a learner. Earn the respect of your coworkers; don't demand it. Maintain a quiet sense of confidence, and don't be afraid to learn from everyone. Expect even the lowest person on the totem pole to have something valuable to teach you.

When your head gets too big to fit through the door, remember where you came from. Don't rub it in or flaunt it in front of your coworkers and friends.

—**Bradley G. Richardson,** ***Jobsmarts for Twentysomethings***

KNOW WHEN TO FOLLOW

If you have a problem with authority, you better work on resolving it now. Even if your parents allowed constant questioning and your instructor enjoyed your challenges, your boss won't. Save your challenges for the big issues, not the daily demands of your job. Learn how to follow.

How do you follow a boss who seems like an idiot? You salute the uniform. Respect the position. Never try to show her up in public or diminish her authority. Part of your job is to make your boss look good.

A good follower pays attention when other team members talk. No matter how boring a meeting might be, take notes instead of filing or chewing your nails. You may not think anyone notices what you do in meetings, but they do. If you're the only one establishing eye contact with the speaker, you'll be remembered.

Being a follower doesn't mean keeping your mouth shut and sitting on your hands. There's a time for everything under the sun—a time to support the

A GOOD FOLLOWER . . .

- makes the boss look good
- carefully chooses his or her times of disagreement
- supports team ideas
- asks for advice
- gives full attention when others speak
- follows orders
- offers solutions, not problems

A GOOD LEADER . . .

- volunteers for responsibility
- acts on his or her own initiative
- takes input from others and makes decisions
- contributes in the most helpful way to the team
- takes personal responsibility for team goals
- tries to motivate teammates
- admits when he or she is wrong
- is willing to follow others when necessary

ideas of others and a time to contribute your own ideas. Don't feel you have to give your opinion on everything. Pick the most meaningful opportunities, and communicate clearly in as few words as possible.

All good leaders were once good followers.

DON'T THINK TOO LOWLY OF YOURSELF

Humility means not thinking too highly of yourself, but it also means not thinking too lowly of yourself. Just as you should be realistic about your weaknesses, don't shy away from using your strengths. Know exactly what you have to offer your company that nobody else has.

Just because you're trying to learn as much as possible, don't hold back your talents. Try to share them with others. While people may or may not want to utilize your talents, your offer says good things about how you present yourself to others. Don't pretend to know less than you do.

KNOW WHEN TO LEAD

During your first year, you will probably be more of a follower than a leader. But be ready to lead whenever it helps the team. Leadership means taking responsibility, not credit. Volunteer for jobs that will help your team. Fulfill every responsibility, no matter how small, and your team will come to depend on you.

Accept yourself realistically and visualize your own potential. Learn all you can, including what you gather from your own mistakes. Start accepting yourself so you'll have no need to prove yourself to yourself. Become someone you like and trust.

EXERCISE

- Take an honest look at your last semester in school. List five of the best and five of the worst things about you during that period.
- Do you tend to think too highly or too lowly of yourself? Explain.
- Celebrate your successes. List 10 things you did last week that you feel good about (for example, completed an English assignment or listened to a friend).
- Name three things or processes you'd like to learn this year.

IN SUMMARY . . .

- Know when to lead and when to follow at work. Stand by and carefully observe so you are ready to lead when the time comes.
- Keep learning about your company every day and never stop asking questions.
- Have a positive attitude and volunteer for duties—this will show employers your commitment to the job.
- Be humble at work, but don't think too lowly of yourself.
- Take good notes and encourage your coworkers.
- Part of your job is to make your boss look good. Do this by being a good listener, learning the duties of your coworkers, and being a professional representative of your company.

7

IMPROVE YOUR TIME-MANAGEMENT, GOAL-SETTING, AND MEMORY SKILLS

"What I really need is more time."
"There just aren't enough hours in the day!"
"Where did the time go?"
"She just isn't giving us enough time."

Do these quotes sound like things you say often? In general, people complain about time more than anything else. Yet time is one of the few things that we all receive in equal amounts on a daily basis. If you're not getting cheated out of the amount of time you get and you still feel like you don't have enough, that leaves just one explanation: You're not managing your time well.

FACT

Microsoft asked 1,000 businesspeople to identify the most important factor for financial success. Only 32 percent got the right answer: having clearly defined goals.

THE TYRANNY OF THE URGENT

Cal knew he should have studied for his Spanish test last night, but at least he had a study hall before class. He sat down and started to open his book.

"Cal," Nora said, easing beside him. "You have to help me with my algebra."

Cal took one look at the beautiful Nora and knew Spanish could wait long enough to rescue her. Ten minutes later Nora closed her algebra book, thanked Cal, and walked away.

Cal rallied himself. He still had 35 minutes to study—plenty of time. He opened his text to the Spanish vocabulary page, but was interrupted by the PA system: "Anybody trying out for track, meet the coach in the gym for a five-minute briefing."

Cal had to go. It was track, after all, and it wouldn't take long. He'd still have time to study when he got back. Ten minutes later, Cal returned to study hall and found a note from his girlfriend. Somebody had gotten word to her that he'd been flirting with Nora. He had to straighten out that misunderstanding right away.

As Cal sidled over to his girlfriend's table, he was stopped by the art teacher—something about cleaning up his mess in the art room . . . now! While wiping the last dried glob of red paint from the art room chalkboard, the bell rang. It was time for Spanish.

Cal was suffering from "the tyranny of the urgent." Some of us live our lives without a plan, bouncing from one urgent demand to another. In the business world, you're going to have times of hectic pace and urgencies that demand your attention. Your job is to stay in control.

Have you ever watched people ski? Beginners tumble at the mercy of the hill. The novice controls his descent by fighting the hill, braking all the way. But the expert skier goes with the hill, controlling his own movement. He's not afraid to run out of control. He enjoys the speed of the hill, because he knows he can resume control when he needs too. That's what you need to do in the fast-lane of the business world. Enjoy the ride and go with it when you want to, but know that you can pull out when you need to. Otherwise you'll go down in the drift of things that have to get done this minute. You'll never get to important-but-not-urgent tasks. And you'll hate the ride.

To keep your head up out there:

- Get your priorities straight.
- Set personal goals.
- Plan and schedule your activities.

Time is the most precious element of human existence. The successful person knows how to put energy into time and how to draw success from time.

—Denis Waitley, American author and motivational speaker

GET YOUR PRIORITIES STRAIGHT

Start by listing the things that are most important to you. Some factors to weigh and consider are the amount of time you spend with your friends versus your boyfriend or girlfriend, your summer job versus your summer beach plans, and the amount of time you need to devote to both schoolwork and extracurricular activities in the coming year. Once you have a list of issues, start determining your priorities by placing the most important items—the items that need your attention most—near the top. Once you establish your list of priorities, you are ready to start setting goals.

BOOKS ON GOAL SETTING

Bachel, Beverly K. *What Do You Really Want? How to Set a Goal and Go For It! A Guide for Teens.* Minneapolis, Minn.: Free Spirit Publishing, 2001.

Blair, George Ryan. *Goal Setting 101: How to Set and Achieve a Goal!* Palm Harbor, Fla.: The GoalsGuy, 2000.

Gable, Cate. *Strategic Action Planning Now! A Guide for Setting and Meeting Your Goals.* Port Saint Lucie, Fla.: Saint Lucie Press, 1998.

Smith, Douglas K. *Make Success Measurable!: A Mindbook-Workbook for Setting Goals and Taking Action.* New York: John Wiley & Sons, 1999.

SETTING PERSONAL GOALS

Have you noticed that if you don't plan things, they don't get done? You may really want to learn the guitar. But until you transform that desire and priority into a workable goal, you'll be singing a cappella.

Goals come in all sizes, from large life goals such as finding your dream job to daily goals such as making your bed. If you've never set goals before, it might be worth your time to jot down a general life goal in each of the following major areas of your life:

- Family
- Financial
- Intellectual
- Physical
- Social
- Spiritual
- Vocational
- Other

For example, a long-range or life goal in the social area might be: "to be at ease and functional in every kind of social situation." A financial goal might be: "to be debt free, with enough money to buy necessities and be free from money worries" or "to be a billionaire."

Goals define our mission in life. Without goals, we have no criteria to judge each job or career change.

—Amy Lindgren, president and founder of Prototype Career Services

SHORT-TERM GOALS

Your initial goals should be short-term specific. This will help you work on your larger life goals in a more organized manner. Try setting up goals for one semester. Now you get to chip away at a piece of that life goal.

For example, realistic financial goals for this semester might be:

- Get a part-time job.
- Save $200 this semester.
- Pay my brother back his $75.

Other goals for the semester might include:

- Raise my geometry grade one letter.
- Pass chemistry.
- Make the honor roll.
- Be on time to class every day.
- Study for tests.
- Keep my locker organized.
- Get a role in the play.
- Get along with coach.

Your next step is to break up your goals into parts or steps, called *objectives*. If you fulfill each objective, you'll reach your goal. For instance, decide on several steps that will enable you to save $200 by the end of the semester, such as taking a babysitting job after school or putting aside $30 each week and depositing it in the bank. Do this with each goal, breaking it down into manageable steps. Now you have a plan of action.

SCHEDULE THE PLAN

So far you have goals, objectives, and plans. But you need also to accomplish these items within a certain time period. Say you've made it your goal to study more for tests this semester. To accomplish that goal, you need to make a weekly schedule, as seen in the following exercise.

Guard well your spare moments. They are like uncut diamonds. Discard them and their value will never be known.

—Ralph Waldo Emerson, American writer

AVOID PROCRASTINATION

You have goals, objectives, a plan, and a schedule. Now all you have to do is fulfill them. And the only thing that can get in your way is procrastination.

EXERCISE

Weekly Planner

Time	Monday	Tuesday	Wednesday	Thursday	Friday	Saturday	Sunday
6:00 A.M.							
7:00 A.M.							
8:00 A.M.							
9:00 A.M.							
10:00 A.M.							
11:00 A.M.							
12:00 P.M.							
1:00 P.M.							
2:00 P.M.							
3:00 P.M.							
4:00 P.M.							
5:00 P.M.							
6:00 P.M.							
7:00 P.M.							
8:00 P.M.							
9:00 P.M.							
10:00 P.M.							
11:00 P.M.							
12:00 A.M.							

Now, schedule, schedule, schedule! Write the givens: school, work hours, sleep, and your favorite TV show. Then schedule activities you've worked out in your short-term goals. If you study from seven to nine on Monday and Tuesday nights, you know you'll have time to prep for tests. Look at your syllabi and plan extra study nights for scheduled exams.

Write in your exercise times and when you'll weigh in to see how you're doing. And don't forget to schedule fun. Capture time and use it the way you want to.

Procrastination is the habit of putting off until tomorrow . . . and the next day . . . and the day after . . . . It's a good habit to break.

Although there's no proven cure for procrastination, it might help to keep in mind the following tips:

- Evaluate your current schedule and find out where you're wasting your time.
- If fear of failure is holding you back, admit it.
- Make yourself accountable to another person. Ask a friend or family member to ask you if you're keeping up with your goals. This will keep you motivated.
- Is your problem starting a project? Schedule an exact time to begin.
- Is your problem finishing? Set up a system of checks and balances. (Create a chart where you write down your weight every Friday; a joint work session when you'll have to show someone how much you've done.)
- Break the big picture into less-threatening steps.
- Reward yourself at various stages. (If you read 50 pages, you get a bowl of ice cream—unless, of course, you're also trying to lose weight!)
- Celebrate the little victories along the way.

- Get a partner, someone with a similar goal.
- Give your goal a reality check. If you've never run a mile, you're probably shooting too high to enter a marathon.

MEMORY SKILLS

Just as you can manage your time with a little work and planning, you can learn to manage your memory. If you want to excel in business, a good memory can be an incredible asset.

If you want to excel in business, a good memory can be an incredible asset.

David learned about memory the hard way. In his first month in telemarketing, he called his boss by the wrong name, forgot where he put his employee manual, spaced out during an early morning meeting, and forgot an important client's identity. While all of this was bad enough, there was more.

David explains: "I knew I was supposed to ship documents to Portland, Maine. But it slipped my mind. I sent a major shipment to Portland, Oregon. That was the last straw. I knew I needed to improve my memory."

David read a book, practiced, and improved his memory. Generally, memory consists of three elements: acquiring, storing, and recalling. Most of us have our biggest problems with recall. There are many techniques out there to help you manage your memory. We'll take a look at a few of the simplest.

FACT

Napoleon III boasted that in spite of all his royal duties he could remember the name of every person he met. He had people repeat their names and sometimes spell them. Then he associated their names with other things.

Listen Up

Probably the simplest memory aid is to improve your listening. Pay attention when someone gives you her name. When you're about to receive an important piece of information, stop what you're doing and give your full attention. If you're not sure you understand the information, ask to have it repeated.

Write It Down

Make use of lists and calendars. Use a personal organizer or create a database that includes meeting times and dates. Check your calendar every day. If you have a good organizational system, you won't have to remember so much.

Make one central "to-do" list and refer to it often. If you're supposed to remember to file a report, to drop off some papers, and to pick up supplies, jot these things down on today's to-do list. Make a point to look at it at least two times a day so you don't neglect or forget about important responsibilities.

Word Association

Say you want to remember your shopping list: eggs, butter, garlic, spaghetti, and dog food. Try to make an unforgettable association with the words: You're using a stick of *butter* as a skateboard, racing down the sidewalk, your *dog* barking along behind. Your hair has turned to *spaghetti*, streaming in the wind. You're holding a raw *egg* in each outstretched arm. And passersby cross the street because of your *garlic* breath. Now there's a picture that's harder to forget than your

SURF THE WEB:
IMPROVE YOUR MEMORY

Brain Dance.com
http://braindance.com/bdimem1.htm

Mind Tools.com
http://www.mindtools.com/memory.html

Premium Heath.com
http://www.premiumhealth.com/memory/htiym.htm

Wanna Learn.com
http://www.wannalearn.com/Personal_Enrichment/Improve_Your_Memory

original list. And you should be able to pick out the items you need. You've associated them with a vivid picture.

I always have trouble remembering three things: faces, names, and—I can't remember what the third thing is.

—Fred A. Allen, American radio comic

Visualization

If you can picture what you want to remember, you'll have a better chance at remembering it. Imagine Ms. Leopard in a leopard-skin coat; Mr. Brown dressed totally in brown; Ms. Cratchet with a ratchet. Sometimes, the more offbeat the image, the easier it is to remember.

FACT

According to psychologists, the "short-term memory" is the working memory, capable of recording seven items for a maximum of 30 seconds. An example is holding a phone number in your mind long enough to dial it.

Mnemonics

Mnemonics are tricks to help you remember. You can use alliteration (mean Mrs. Masters made me mad).

Or simple repetition and rhyme might help your memory: "Use legs, get eggs."

Acronyms are words that help you remember several items that start with the letters of the acronyms: BEAT=butter, eggs, apple, toast. HOMES=Huron, Ontario, Michigan, Erie, Superior (the Great Lakes).

You can make up your own code to help you spell a name correctly: Treit=That rat eats ice, too. Or you can memorize the names and order of the planets by making up a sentence using words that begin with the first letters as planet names: My (Mercury) very (Venus) elderly (Earth) mother (Mars) just

TIPS FOR REMEMBERING NAMES

- Pay attention!
- Repeat the name aloud.
- Write the name down when the person leaves.
- Make a rhyme: Matt Spry=Fat Guy.
- Make up a visual image of the person connected with his name: Mr. Mallard riding a duck.
- Make an acrostic of the name: Mrs. Hales=Horrible aliens let eagles sing.

(Jupiter) served (Saturn) us (Uranus) nine (Neptune) pizzas (Pluto).

Manage your memory and manage your time, and you'll be way ahead of the game when you start your new career.

Professionalism: It's NOT the job you DO; it's HOW you DO the job.

—Anonymous

EXERCISE

- **Keep a time chart of what you do throughout one day. Include everything: "3:05 to 4:10, talked with friends; 4:10 to 5:30, watched TV . . . ."**
- **Develop a pie chart that reflects how you use your time.**
- **List your top five time wasters.**
- **Decide on one thing you want to accomplish tomorrow, something you just haven't seemed to be able to get done. Draw up a schedule and schedule that activity. Do the activity.**

(continues)

IN SUMMARY . . .

- To improve your memory; use techniques including word association, mnemonics, and visualization. In addition, listen carefully and write important information down to boost your memory skills.
- Set long-term and short-term goals for yourself. Break them into manageable parts and make sure they are specific.

EXERCISE

(continued)

- **Without using any memory "tricks," see how many items you can memorize on this list: turkey, ring, car, tomato, basket, cheese, pencil. Give yourself five minutes to read the list and commit it to memory. (Remember, no tricks.)**
- **Do something else for five minutes. Then see how many you remember. Wait 20 minutes and try again.**
- **Make up a mental picture, a visual that includes all the items (a turkey carrying a basket. . .). Give yourself a memory check after five minutes and after 20 minutes. You should be able to remember all the items now.**

- You will have much more time for leisure, and you will get more done if prioritize and cut out procrastination.

8

MAINTAIN BALANCE TO SUCCEED IN THE WORKPLACE

Ever notice how life is filled with contradictions? You're told to relax but to be on guard; to trust people but to watch your back; to be nice but to not let people walk all over you; to live for the moment but to plan for the future; to have confidence that you can do anything but to be realistic about your limitations. Do these expectations seem difficult to balance?

That's life. It's a balancing act. This book has covered a lot of areas you can work on to get ready for a great career. But none of it will do you much good if you're too stressed on the job to enjoy your life.

We'll close with some tips provided by people who have learned about stress and self-esteem on the job. The material that follows comes from interviews with first-year and second-year employees in a wide range of careers and positions—from investors to truckers, airline attendants to news reporters.

FACT

According to the *Winter 2003 Salary Survey,* conducted by the National Association of Colleges and Employees, the average starting salary for the following majors are as follows:

- **Accounting: $42,005**
- **Business: $36,634**
- **Civil engineering: $41,541**
- **Computer engineering: $52,722**
- **Computer science: $44,678**
- **Criminal justice: $27,596**
- **Economics: $40,413**
- **English: $35,538**
- **Liberal arts/general studies: $29,586**
- **Management information systems: $40,566**
- **Marketing: $35,698**
- **Political science: $34,594**
- **Psychology: $27,194**
- **Social work: $26,459**

Source: Jobweb.com (http://www.jobweb.com)

UNREASONABLE EXPECTATIONS

Be realistic—you're not going to come in like a Broadway star and wow the corporation your first week. You probably won't get a raise your first year. Nobody will pat you on the back for coming in on time and doing what they hired you to do. Your first employee evaluation may be lukewarm.

When you come in with too many unreasonable expectations, you set yourself up for stress and

TOP CAUSES OF JOB STRESS

- Unreasonable job expectations
- Lack of preparation
- Financial problems
- Lack of self-forgiveness
- Inflexibility
- Unhappiness outside the office
- Personality clashes
- Lack of job knowledge or skill
- No outside interest or life outside of work
- Poor self-image

disappointment. Remember that your first year is a time to learn. Let your employer teach you. Be like a sponge and take in as much as you can. Have fun getting smart. There will be plenty of time to wow them somewhere down the road.

BE PREPARED

Those Boy Scouts know what they're talking about. Being prepared for any situation is an invaluable asset. Andrew pulled As and Bs in high school and college with little effort. He says, "I could always wing it when I had to give a speech or report."

Then he got his job with a research team in California. He said, "The first time I had to present findings, I tried to wing it. I got so nervous the morning of our meeting, I could barely talk."

Don't "wing it" on the job. Prepare. Overprepare until you don't have to think about what you'll say. Solid preparation is one of the surest ways to relieve job stress and to take the pressure off.

THE POWER OF WORKING HARD

You might think you'll have a better chance of escaping job stress if you don't work so hard. But usually the opposite is true. There is power in knowing you've done your very best.

When you work hard and do your best, you don't have to kick yourself when something goes wrong. You can at least know that you did what you could. And others will know it, too.

FACT

According to GLS Consulting Inc., 44 percent of employees surveyed said their on-the-job stress had worsened since the terrorist attacks of September 11, 2001—in part because of the threat of layoffs. In addition, 62 percent of those polled said poor communication in the workplace had caused increased levels of stress.

ROLL WITH THE PUNCHES

Nobody can predict the future. Your job will probably not be exactly what you expected. And just when you get the hang of it, it will change. You have to learn to change with it.

Learn to be flexible. If you stubbornly resist change or show your resentment every time you have to shift directions, you'll be considered hard to work with. So relax. You can't stop the changes, so you might as well be a good sport. Besides, you will probably want a promotion at some point, in which case you know your job will change. The sooner you show your adaptability to changes, the better your chances will be for advancement.

The more you learn about your job and everybody else's jobs, the better off you'll be. Ask questions. Be versatile. Make a name for yourself as someone who can fill in almost anywhere. If your company downsizes and lays people off, you'll be someone they can't afford to let go. If they phase out your position, they know you'll fit in anywhere.

MARK YOUR SUCCESSES

Most of us pay a lot more attention to our failures than to our successes. But if you want to build your self-esteem, give yourself credit for the little successes along the way.

If you get to work early every day for a week and if that's an accomplishment for you, pat yourself on the back. You deserve credit. If you know you did your best and did more than was required of you that day, good for you. Celebrate your success. If you keep a journal, write down your victories.

ADMIT YOUR MISTAKES

Job stress is usually at its highest when you make a mistake. Everybody will make mistakes on the job.

How you handle your mistakes will determine your level of stress.

First, try to keep a positive perspective. Try to view your mistakes in comparison with all the things you've done right. Don't keep focusing on the mistake and interpreting everything around you in light of that error. It's just a small part of a much bigger picture.

It's also important to own up to your mistakes. Don't try to shift the blame or waste time trying to explain yourself and justify what you know is wrong. Do what you need to do—admit it and apologize. Try to lessen the fallout.

Forgive yourself first. If you don't, the mistake will stick with you, making you afraid to take the necessary risks your job requires. You can paralyze yourself with indecision. Instead, accept it and move on. You're okay and just as smart and capable as you ever were.

Learn from your mistakes. There may be no better teacher than to make a mistake and learn from it. So don't waste a golden opportunity by reveling in self-pity.

There may be no better teacher than to make a mistake and learn from it.

HAVE A SENSE OF HUMOR

Finally, learn to laugh at yourself. Over and over, men and women reported that a healthy sense of humor is the best stress reliever.

It is important to have interests outside of work, such as a hobby like mountain biking. They will help you maintain balance and fulfill personal needs in your life. (Corbis)

Find the humor in every stressful situation. And make sure that humor is directed toward you, not toward someone else. A good sense of humor can restore perspective, defuse tense negotiations, and patch up bruised relationships.

They say the seeds of what we will do are in all of us, but it always seemed to me that in those who make jokes in life the seeds are covered with better soil and with a higher grade of manure.

—Ernest Hemingway, American writer

MAINTAIN BALANCE

Balanced individuals have a life outside the workplace. Keep your home life in order; make your home a place of refuge and relaxation. Have a hobby to

NEEDS YOUR JOB PROBABLY WON'T FULFILL

- Your need for a best friend
- Exercise
- Fun
- Spiritual fulfillment
- Relaxation
- Emotional release

pursue for entertainment. Give yourself outside events and engagements to look forward to, especially when you're not looking forward to going to work. Take care of yourself with healthy eating, ample sleep, and regular exercise.

Don't try to get all your needs fulfilled through your work. Your life is more than what you do. Start now to work on your self-development. Follow a professional code of ethics. Perfect your etiquette. Become the kind of person you'd hire if you were the boss. Become the kind of person you'd like to be.

IN SUMMARY . . .

- Balance your work life and your home life, and don't expect your job to fulfill all of your needs.
- Have realistic expectations when you start at a new job. Don't get upset if your first year isn't as fulfilling as you'd hoped—you'll get more responsibilities eventually.
- Learn to roll with the punches and realize that your job probably won't be what you expected.
- To find career success, always work hard and treat others as you would like to be treated.

GLOSSARY

acronyms: made-up words or groups of letters people use to help remember several items starting with those letters; may also be referred to as an acrostic

aggressively nice: thoughtful and considerate, acting on and following through with thoughtfulness

choleric: one of the four temperaments; confident, usually goal-oriented and capable

ethics: a system of morals; the code of unwritten rules about how we act toward others

etiquette: the unwritten rules of good manners and taste

extrovert: outgoing; people who enjoy and are at ease in crowds and in new situations

humility: thinking accurately about oneself—not too highly and not too lowly

initiative: the act of taking the first step or making the first move

interpersonal skill: the measure of one's ability to interact with other people

introvert: the tendency to keep to oneself rather than seeking other people

learning style: an individual's preferred method for acquiring information

manners: the means by which we put the rules that we live by into effect

melancholy: one of the four temperaments; usually artistic, organized, analytical, and sensitive

mentor: an unofficial teacher, coach, or adviser

mnemonics: tricks to help remember; to aid recall through rhyme, alliteration, repetition, etc.

objectives: the specific things you hope to accomplish when you set goals

personality inventory: a scientific test designed to help people pinpoint their personality types, as well as their strengths and weaknesses

phlegmatic: one of the four temperaments; generally easygoing, well-balanced, steady

procrastination: the act of putting tasks off until "tomorrow"

sanguine: one of the four temperaments; outgoing, lively, and popular

self-discovery: the process of evaluating and observing yourself to gain self-knowledge

self-knowledge: knowledge of one's personal and professional characteristics, strengths, weaknesses, etc.

short-term memory: the working memory, which is capable of retaining information for a maximum of 30 seconds

temperament: one's nature or customary frame of mind and natural disposition

thinking style: in this book, a description of one's innate tendencies toward a personality style; one is born with an introverted or extroverted way of thinking

values: the things and principles most important to us

visualization: a memory technique that involves creating a mental picture of what is being said

word association: in this book, a memory technique that involves assigning a fictional meaning to a group of words so as to relate them to one another

work ethic: a system of values where much importance is ascribed to working hard

BIBLIOGRAPHY

Balzano, Frederica J., and Marsha Boone Kelly. *Why Should Extroverts Make All the Money? Networking Made Easy for the Introvert.* New York: McGraw-Hill/Contemporary Books, 1999.

Bixler, Susan. *Professional Presence: The Total Program for Gaining That Extra Edge in Business by America's Top Corporate Image Consultant.* Collingdale, Pa.: DIANE Publishing, 1991.

Camenson, Blythe. *Careers for Introverts and Other Solitary Types.* New York: McGraw-Hill/Contemporary Books, 1998.

Fischgrund, Tom. *The Insider's Guide to the Top 20 Careers in Business and Management: What It's Really Like to Work in Advertising, Computers, Banking, Management, and Many More!* New York: McGraw-Hill Trade, 1993.

Kinlaw, Dennis C. *Developing Superior Work Teams.* Lanham, Md.: Lexington Books, 1990.

Laney, Marti Olsen. *The Introvert Advantage: Making the Most of Your Hidden Strengths*. New York: Workman Publishing Company, 2002.

Lapp, Danielle C. *Nearly Total Recall*. Stanford, Calif.: Stanford Alumni Association, 1998.

Lorayne, Harry. *How to Develop a Super-Power Memory*. New York: New American Library, 1990.

Raudsepp, Eugene. *Growth Games for the Creative Manager*. New York: Perigree, 1987.

Richardson, Bradley G. *Jobsmarts for Twentysomethings*. New York: Vintage Books, 1995.

Simon, Sidney B., Leland Howe, and Howard Kirschenbaum. *Values Clarification*. New York: Time Warner Books, 1995.

Terkel, Susan Neiburg, and R. Shannon Duval. *Encyclopedia of Ethics*. New York: Facts On File, 1999.

Vance, Sandra S., and Roy V. Scott. *Wal-Mart: A History of Sam Walton's Retail Phenomenon*. New York: Twayne Publishers, 1994.

Index